MUDVILLE DIARIES

MUDVILLE

A BOOK OF BASEBALL MEMORIES

COLLECTED BY MIKE SCHACHT

DIARIES

AVON BOOKS ◆ NEW YORK

MUDVILLE DIARIES is an original publication of Avon Books. This work has never before appeared in book form.

AVON BOOKS
A division of
The Hearst Corporation
1350 Avenue of the Americas
New York, New York 10019

Copyright © 1996 by *Fan* magazine
Published by arrangement with the editor
Library of Congress Catalog Card Number: 95-38966
ISBN: 0-380-72632-7

Library of Congress Cataloging in Publication Data:
Mudville diaries : a book of baseball memories / collected by Mike Schacht.
     p.   cm.
     1. Baseball—United States—Miscellanea.   I. Schacht, Mike.
GV863.A1M83 1996   95-38966
796.357'0973—dc20   CIP

First Avon Books Trade Printing: March 1996

This book is dedicated to Bill Schacht.

One summer day more than fifty years ago he had no one to play catch with. Dejected yet determined, he invited his younger brother to play. Thus my introduction to baseball. It happened in our backyard in Cincinnati, Ohio, which, appropriately, is the birthplace of professional baseball.

Thanks, William.

Mike Schacht

Acknowledgments

I was teaching baseball courses at the New School for Social Research when I discovered everyone has a baseball story. That discovery inspired the creation of *Fan* magazine, and more than one thousand contributors and eighteen issues later, this book was born. Thanks to all those contributors and special thanks to my *Fan* colleagues: editors John Simonson, Elinor Nauen and Margery Kimbrough; design director Tony Palladino; and Jim McKibben, Ron Williams, and Chris Jennison. Thanks to my three daughters, Wendy, Sallie, and Margot for supporting their dad's crazy career, and to my partner, Linda, for her unfailing belief in my work. Finally, thanks to Ivy Fischer Stone of the Oscard Agency and Stephen S. Power of Avon Books.

Mike Schacht

MUDVILLE DIARIES

When I went to my first baseball game my father dropped the pencil he was keeping score with. He asked me to climb down to get it and while I was under the seat I missed Frank Torre hit a grand-slam home run.

Mark Fuller

My father took me to see my first baseball game in 1948. I was only six years old, but I already knew a lot about the game because we were the first ones in our building to have a television set, and whenever a game was on all of our neighbors would pile into our living room to watch and talk about baseball. Other than Howdy Doody and boxing, there wasn't much else to watch on television in those days.

My first baseball game was at night at Ebbets Field in Brooklyn, and I can still remember holding my father's hand and coming out of a dark tunnel-like ramp into the middle of a huge screaming crowd lit by banks of brilliant bulbs outlined against the dark sky. I think I must have expected to see tiny TV-sized men playing on a gray field because when I saw the incredibly bright green grass I nearly fainted.

We had seats that were practically on the field, and when the players came out of the dugout I was shocked to see how tall they were and how white the beautiful Dodger uniforms looked with their royal blue script logo and bright red numbers. Jackie Robinson, my favorite player, stood right in front of us on the field and I was sure he smiled at me. I had two hot dogs, a bag and a half of peanuts, a Coke and then a Dixie Cup, and I finally threw up so we had to leave before the end of the game. But I'll never forget that night and thinking that there was nothing as much fun in the world as going to a real live game.

Mara Kurtz

Everything I remember about those summers is built on the nasal twang of Mel Allen calling the plays. During my adolescence in the middle fifties, his voice was synonymous with summer. *It's a high fly to right field,* he would almost sing. It was in the background of everything. It was the Yankees, always, a doubleheader, the game extending into radio time forever and ever. At the lake the radio from the snack bar projected his voice out over the beach and slapped at you, the wake from a motorboat out near the center of the lake, a delayed slap, slap, slap.

Helen Ruggieri

On summer evenings after supper my older brother and I would play catch in our yard. The coolness of evening would begin to descend from the hills surrounding us, and the world seemed composed only of a white ball going back and forth across a green lawn. Though we must have done this hundreds of times, they now all seem lumped together into one single moment, a moment that defined the first half of my childhood, as if time itself crystallized around one specific memory. In the purity of my nine-year-old mind, I thought the world would never change.

David Appell

That summer my father taught me to throw a baseball. We threw in the side yard where nobody could see us—not Rhoda, not Nina, and certainly not any boys. I didn't even know how to hold the ball at first.

Dad would toss me easy catches, giving me confidence, gradually putting more on his throws. "Keep your eye on the ball," he said. I imagined that I was a pitcher on a Little League Team. Soon I started to throw the ball where I wanted it to go. My control was good, my father said. I became good at twenty feet, then forty. I liked being the pitcher.

One night Nina, Rhoda, and I made our familiar trek to the ballfield to watch a Little League game. We were earlier than usual and the teams were just warming up. We walked along the right field line toward the snack hut. A foul ball sailed through the night air toward us. For a moment I thought of trying to catch it, but I had no glove, and I stepped back. The ball bounced and rolled to a stop in front of us. Before I knew what I was doing I had the ball in my hand. Nina and Rhoda looked mortified; we never picked up foul balls.

I saw the coach who was following the ball, and he saw me. He looked very small, and I suddenly had the feeling that I was standing deep in the outfield and he was the second baseman. I'd never be accurate, I thought, or get anything on the ball. Then I imagined the runner had reached third and was trying to make it home.

The ball left my hand. Maybe Nina and Rhoda watched the flight; I didn't. I shut my eyes. I heard the coach call out, *"Nice arm, kid!"*

Hillary Homzie

My father was a very difficult man, full of frustration and anger. His outlet was yelling. Baseball became more than something I grew up to love and appreciate—it became a great shield for me. Whenever my father revved up for a good holler, I would say, "Let's watch a baseball game." At a baseball game everyone yells—at umpires, players, managers, other fans. It is part of the spirit of an afternoon at the ballpark. What could be better than giving my father a target different from me?

Years later I found a way to forgive him for his yelling. He had, within the quieter moments of his angry existence, taught me baseball.

Linda Ayache

James Crnkovich

Every time I see a baseball game, I'm reminded of the day Mother played with us. It happened a long time ago, but that was still the fastest ball I ever saw, or didn't see.

My mother was a great sport, but baseball wasn't her game. She always used the same excuse. "I couldn't hit the ball if it was on the bat," she said. And we believed her. Yet we wanted her to try, and we kept pestering her with, "Please, Ma, just once. Please, maybe you'll hit it." Finally, she gave us our wish.

We had a big yard. My sister Aggie and I were on the school team and we needed all the extra practice we could get. That's why we wanted Mother to play. We wanted to perfect our pitching and catching techniques.

I was pitcher, Ag catcher. Our faces split into grins, anxious to see how she would handle the first pitch. She held the bat as though it were an everyday habit. She looked so natural in that spot. I hurled a straight ball. It was a perfect pitch. Mother swung beautifully. The ball shot straight back to me, but before I could raise a glove, I was out of today and wandering on the edge of forever after. Smack in the forehead. When I came to, Mother was cradling my head in her arms.

Still caressing my head, half crying, half scolding us for what we made her do, she vowed to never play baseball again. And she never did. We often teased her about playing, but she would just squint and give us a sidelong glance and we'd break into laughter.

That was all a long time ago, but I'm reminded of it every base-ball season.

Margaret Malinoske

When I was growing up my father attended most of my games. On those rare occasions when he missed one, his questions were always the same. First, "Who won the game?" Then, "How did you do?" If I got a hit, and I usually did, it would be, "Was it a clean hit?" To this day, I often find myself using that same kind of distinction.

Mike Schacht

Our Yankee Stadium:
the October cornfield bordered
backyard diamond where my son
with teeth clenched
squeezes the bat,
waiting for my smoke.
I fire toward the bat lashing out;
the ball flies toward the apple tree.
It clears the tree and the fence
and drops into Indian summer's
dried corn stalks,
crackling like the explosive cheers
of bleacher fans.
Leaves spin like confetti
to honor his longest home run
in four years of batting against me.
I will have to bear down
as middle age nears,
to convince him that I'm still
the best pitcher around.

Gene Fehler

After the game we jumped down onto the outfield grass from our bleacher seats. In the old days the fans could walk across the field to get out of Yankee Stadium. There was lots of activity—people [were] moving in all directions. Dodging them was part of *our* game, along with make-believe throws, home-run swings, slides, swooping tags.

Today I had a plan. I was keeping an eye on the exact spot where DiMaggio always stood in center field. The moving crowd kept blocking my view and I had to concentrate. As I moved closer to the spot I felt scared, and a little embarrassed. *Geez, someone's gonna see me do it.*

I ripped up a handful of grass and dirt from the spot and flew it into my pocket. Didn't tell anyone about it, ever. Kept it in a white envelope marked "Joe D."

Tony Palladino

We had an intercom system with a radio connecting the rooms in our house. Every night during baseball season my brothers and I would lie in our beds and listen to a game until we fell asleep. It was my father's version of a bedtime story.

Ann Batdorf

I dream the bat's too heavy. It's a thick-handled #5 Mickey Mantle rather than my lean #4 Johnny Bench, which I must have split the week before, and its leaden weight deadens my muscles, aggravates the soreness of my joints. Following a few clumsy swings, I drape the bat over my shoulders like a yoke and approach the plate, eyes on the turf. Gripping the bat at the base of the handle, I'm unable to control its balance, the tip falling to the ground with a thud. I shorten my grip and with difficulty lift the bat to my shoulder, and as I step into the box I look up to find playing the field against me the entire army of the People's Republic of China equipped with mitts the size of peach baskets. I step aside to wipe the sweat from my hands, then, gathering all my strength, take one last, ferocious swing. The left side of the infield—three hundred thousand strong—retreats a pace, and I return to the plate. The first pitch arches toward me, soft and feathery like a dove, and as if it were indeed a fragile creature buoyed by the air, I tap it lightly across the seams. It dribbles slowly down the third base line, just fair, and the Chinese Army falls all over itself as I leg it out to first, safe.

J. Weintraub

*M*anager relieving his pitcher at the mound late in the game:

"You apparently weren't in our last strategy meeting. We didn't agree that our tactic would be to let people on base to set up a triple play. We were more in favor of a plan to strike out each batter as he came to the plate. Hankinson was at that meeting, so I'm going to give him this opportunity. Meanwhile, why don't you call it a day?"

Al Sandvik

My father will tell you how his daughters enriched his life, how we gave him so much in ways that only girls can. I was the tomboy of the family and he taught me how to hit and catch on our dead-end street. I remember how his eyes would fill each time I stove my finger playing catch.

Lisa Chewning

On June 8, 1968, the Phillies were playing the Dodgers at Dodger Stadium and Don Drysdale pitched his fifty-eighth consecutive scoreless inning, breaking Walter Johnson's record. In another part of Los Angeles, Robert Kennedy's body was being loaded on a plane bound for Washington.

Esther Manes

It was my first visit to Cooperstown and we were in the Hall of Fame Gallery. Sunlight streamed through tall windows. Approaching the immaculate white walls lined with the bronze plaques of immortalized ballplayers, I held my breath. A spontaneous hush fell over us. Then a young boy innocently interrupted our reverie. "Why's everybody so quiet?" he asked his father in a loud voice. He was immediately hushed by his mortified parent. It must have dawned on the poor little guy that he had broken some cardinal rule, for he shamefully bowed his head and stepped back silently, so as not to incur the wrath of the baseball gods.

Joan Thomas

My parents were visiting my wife and me from Florida last October and we all planned to go up to Cooperstown for the weekend. It was raining so heavily Saturday morning that we decided not to go. Saturday night, however, Dad and I got to talking. He too had never been to Cooperstown. We plotted to go, just the two of us, early Sunday morning. We set the alarm and were on the road at 5 A.M. It was cold and foggy, but when the sun finally poked through, the splendor of the fall colors was spectacular.

Doing the entire museum and round-trip all in one day was exhausting, but it was worth it. Dad and I spoke of things we had never discussed before. I don't think I had ever known my father before that day.

Randy Weinberg

After every game at Wrigley Field my friends and I would pester the players for autographs. Quite a few of the big stars would sign a couple of scorecards and then leave the rest of us in their wake as they drove off.

Clyde McCullough was always one of the last to leave for home. I can still picture him signing scorecards on his knee, with his foot propped up on the running board of his Nash. He was a proud, tough man and was reputed to be the last big league catcher to play without a chest protector.

During one such signing session he looked at me and said, "Weren't you here a few times already?"

"Yes, sir," I replied nervously. "I *forgot* about this card I wanted you to sign."

He laughed and rumpled my hair. "Next time bring everything at once. You can save yourself some time." He signed my card and then rode off in his Nash down Waveland Avenue.

Bill De Maria

During the summer I was eleven, poison ivy swelled and blistered the fingers on both my hands. Mom applied ointment and wrapped them snugly in strips of cotton cloth. I could still play ball.

Mr. Spurr, the coach who selected players for our youth league's all-star team, took one look at my hands and virtually ignored me for the rest of the tryouts. We sat in the bleachers as they announced the names of the players selected. I was OK until I got home and saw my mother standing by the kitchen sink. Then I burst into tears.

Life holds small victories. Half the regular season remained and our team played Mr. Spurr's all-stars. On my first at-bat, my hands still bandaged, I caught the ball on the fat of the bat and lined it to left center. The lack of a fence allowed the ball to roll so I legged it out for a homer. As I rounded third I glanced at Mr. Spurr standing by the bench. He looked at me and shrugged his shoulders.

Kevin Grace

I dreamed as a kid of going to the World Series. When the dream was realized in Minnesota in 1987, the best part of the whole thing was being there with the one person in all the world I would have chosen to go with, the man who knows when to look my way. Baseball with my brother is as deep as childhood, as urgent as that charivari in the Decibeldome. With anyone else it could not have been so replete. How did you get seats? people asked. My brother and I go way back, I joked, but it's no quip. We've shared a passion for baseball more consistently and longer than I've shared anything with anybody. Why shouldn't it form part of the core? I see now the unspoken—unconscious—agreement between Charlie and me that we will always be the other's date at that sort of event.

Elinor Nauen

Bill Farrell

He was bigger and stronger then
And you knew he could knock you over
If he really wanted to cut loose
He lobbed at first
And as he threw harder
You knew he was testing you
Seeing what you were made of *today*
Noticing how you handled the stings
Watching how you backpedaled
When he tossed infield flies
He made you run
Firing one wild high or
Bouncing it past your dive
Maybe so he could rest up some
Maybe so you could rest up some
So the game could go on
Till dinnertime or till dark
Or till one of you
Grew up

Gene Carney

I*n life, too, someone has to make the first pitch and someone has to make the final out.*

Anonymous

When I was growing up in the late forties, I was determined to know everything there was to know about the game of baseball. What I never learned were the answers to dozens of questions I wish I had asked my father.

What position did he play? Was he *good?* Who was his favorite big leaguer? Did he ever see Matty, Wagner, or Ruth? Was Walter Johnson really that fast, or Cobb that mean?

I read and enjoy all the oral histories. But for me, none would compare with an interview with my father.

Mike Schacht

June 1969. Mrs. Blumberg's fourth-grade class has earned a trip to Yankee Stadium. "Yea!" Who arranged for Yankee players Jerry Kenney and Gene Michael to shake each little hand in their huge ones? It's a secret.

The boys are thrilled. The girls are in love.

Third inning. A slow grounder squeezes itself under Gene Michael's glove and scurries between his legs into center field. *Oh, dear!* worries Mrs. Blumberg. *Will the children be disillusioned?*

"Isn't he wonderful!" sighs Maria Aviello. "He almost got it!"

Martha Blumberg

My parents probably played catch with me, but I don't remember. I had a glove that was too stiff, and a Tony Oliva bat that was too heavy. The only baseball in the house was autographed—I'd never heard of Phil Rizzuto—and tucked away in my mom's dresser. In the neighborhood we sometimes played whiffleball; more often it was "kick-the-can." I tried out once for Little League. I was cut, humiliated, and never tried again. Our big leaguers, the Kansas City Athletics, had green and gold uniforms and a mule. They lost a lot of games. I remember going once when the Yankees were in town.

The summer after the A's moved away, I played soccer. We were league champions.

John Simonson

I came up to the plate with two out in the last inning of the Loyola High School JV intrasquad game. The last outfield position would go to either Kirk Bridgeforth or me. It came down to one last at bat. I planted my spikes firmly in the batter's box to face the best pitcher in school, Jeff Weyer.

Weyer threw vicious smoke that sailed up as it reached the plate. I fought back by fouling ball after ball against the screen. All I could do was make contact to stay alive. Each time I nicked the ball I would gather myself and dig in again. Weyer wanted to strike me out and finish his stint on the mound without a blemish. I fouled off ten pitches trying to catch up with his heat.

Weyer kicked the rubber and set himself again, unleashing a meteor straight for the center of the plate. I drove the ball deep into center field, a solid rope slicing toward the gymnasium facade. Tommy Fahey reached the asphalt warning track and leaped at the last second, snaring the ball just before it cleared the concrete wall. It was the best ball I hit all spring, the best ball I'd *ever* hit.

The next day I went over to see the listing, confident I had made the team with my final blast. My name wasn't on the list. I went to the locker and cleared out my spikes. From then on I would be taking the early bus home every day, watching from the bus stop as the players warmed up. I had never been cut before.

Three games into the season, Kirk Bridgeforth quit the team. Jeff Weyer never pitched a game at the JV level; he was promoted to varsity as a sophomore.

Whenever I'm going through tough times and doubting myself, I remember that power struggle on that diamond in the dust of sunset, and the triumphant flight of the ball as it screamed toward the gymnasium.

Dean Smith

The one surviving picture of my Little League days shows me in a plain gold cap that stood ridiculously tall on my head. It did so because of my obsession with making the front of the cap stand up, like those of the major leaguers on my baseball cards. Someone showed me how to fold a cap so that the crown would stand tall, not lie flat on my head. Years later while cleaning my room, I found the cap. It was still folded.

Andy Rothman

When my Uncle Jerome, whom I never met, died in World War II, he left behind more than just memories. One of his belongings is so special it has become a cherished family heirloom—a baseball signed by twenty-four members of Joe McCarthy's great Yankee clubs of the late thirties. It's a beautiful ball, a *Reach Official American League* model. *William Harridge, President.* Cushioned cork center. Thick, wide seams. At some point the ball was shellacked to preserve the signatures, though some have aged slightly. Between the seams are the two signatures my uncle prized most, Lou Gehrig and Joe DiMaggio. Today I am the ball's temporary guardian, an honor if there ever was one. It has become a part of my life, and somehow I feel a little closer to an uncle I never knew.

Paul Turner

Joe D. was my first hero. We started our careers together at [Yankee] Stadium, May 3, 1936. The first major league game he played. The first one I saw. He hit a triple that day. I thought it was the most beautiful thing I had witnessed in my eight-year-old life. It's still in my top five.

William Sommer

Mike Schacht

I was born too late. I have no recollection of *the Greatest Ballplayer of All Time.* He was a line in a Paul Simon song. He was Mr. Coffee. I listened to other people's stories and watched those grainy, black-and-white newsreels of a graceful, refined guy in a flannel uniform. But I didn't really know the Joe DiMaggio of American memory.

Then one day I saw him. He was standing alone on a curb in San Francisco, thirty years and 3,000 miles from the Bronx of his well-oiled youth. He stood erect, tweedy, wingtipped; a white-haired warrior waiting as my car flew past like a fastball, high and tight. In the next instant the Yankee Clipper was crossing the street, growing smaller and smaller in my rearview mirror.

John Simonson

As a kid I played my own game of baseball with eighteen different sticks representing various kinds of batters (a thick, stubby stick was number four in the lineup; a thin, stiff one was leadoff, etc.), with extra sticks as pinch hitters, and plenty of pebbles to throw in the air and swat. Certain distances and areas of a vast field were designated as hits or outs—three-baggers, strikeouts, etc.

I'd play for hours by myself.

Sometimes I cheated, a bit, by selecting certain rocks or pebbles of different sizes that I thought might have a better chance of being hit or of going farther when (if) I hit them.

Jack Moore

My father took me to my first baseball game at the old Sportsman's Park when I was six years old. I remember the poles and how difficult it was to see over and around the "big people." Back then most men wore straw hats when they were out in the hot St. Louis sun. The high point was when my father caught a Stan Musial foul ball. He gave the ball to my cousin. Years later I came to resent that.

Glenda Guerri

My father was driving us to our Saturday morning game. We had just stopped to pick up two of my teammates, and we were late for pregame practice. The field where we played was about a fifteen-minute ride.

I was turned to the backseat, talking to my friends, when I felt the car braking quickly, and then a loud thump. We had hit a dog that had run in front of the car.

I've forgotten everything about the game. I'll never forget the sight of my father picking up the dog and carrying it to the owner on his front porch.

Mike Schacht

T he ball game a blur.
The memory there forever.

Don Mir

I never could catch very well, but even as a grade-schooler I could hit. When a little girl is kind of chubbier than she'd like to be, and maybe a bit too bossy for some people's taste, it's a good thing to be able to hit. You hardly ever get picked last.

In high school I went out for the girl's softball team. On the first day of tryouts there were quite a few girls sizing each other up—playing catch, swinging the bat. Arranging us in groups, the coach sent some into the outfield, others to cover the bases, the rest behind the backstop. Strolling to the pitcher's mound she motioned me into the box. I hit all three balls she pitched to me over the center fielder's head—even though she kept backing up.

Despite my weak glove, I made the team. And I *wasn't* the last picked.

Nancy Powers

Last year when I went to Yankee Stadium, the little boy sitting behind me had apparently seen *Field of Dreams* and it must have made a strong impression on him. He asked his father whether he would see Babe Ruth play today. "That would be impossible," his father answered, "because Babe Ruth is dead." Disappointed, the boy replied, "Why should that make any difference?"

Reba Shimansky

It was 1967, the last night of a Red Sox home stand. There were storms in the vicinity, and as the third inning commenced the skies opened. The grounds crew hurried out to roll the tarp across the infield. As they neared second base one of the men fell. People laughed. A slapstick slip in the rain. But the man stayed down. The others gathered around as the first-aid exit opened and two paramedics rushed out. They wheeled the man away and ten minutes later the rain ended; the game resumed. The Sox won. The next day's sports pages described how the sixty-year-old man had collapsed and died. His widow said that perhaps it was fitting, that he had loved the field like a family member.

I was nine. It was the first and only death I have witnessed. I recall that season of the Impossible Dream with great pride, and a touch of sadness. And whenever the rain reaches Fenway and a game is halted, I remember that baseball wasn't the only thing in the summer of 1967.

William Anderson

As a child in Philadelphia I was an ardent A's rooter. The names of Connie Mack and all the players were easier for me to remember than my school lessons. I kept box scores and went to games as often as I could get someone to take me. I even got to see one game in the 1929 World Series against the Cubs. But in the early 1930s the team found its fortunes beginning to fade. Then the move from Philadelphia to Kansas City. My team had gone! Later the A's moved to Oakland and began to win again. While I caught them on TV and read about them in the Philadelphia papers, I never actually saw them play.

A few years ago my son moved to the Bay Area. On a visit there I had the chance to attend an A's game. What a thrill to see the pennants flying, including those won in my childhood!

Then it hit me—of the thirty thousand fans in that ballpark, I was probably the only one who had seen the Athletics win a pennant in Philadelphia sixty years ago.

Leonard K. Lupin

Peewee All Star,
High School MVP,
Billy took the scholarship
packed his glove
for points east.
Came home one year later
with his latest love
four months due.
Found a job
at Nabisco
and faded from view.

Joseph Farley

In 1987 I became a fan of the Minnesota Twins. I liked Gary Gaetti best because he impressed me both on and off the field. I liked his style of play and the way he spoke to the press, the way he went out there to play ball the best that he could.

That same year, I went to the Bronx to see the Twins play the Yanks. I sat high up in the rightfield stands, waving my Homer Hankie (required equipment for Twins fans), trying to ignore the fans taunting the Minnesota outfielders.

After the fifth inning I ran down to field level and poked my head in and out of a few sections before finding the right one. My heart was pounding and my palms sweating, but I made it— first row behind the Twins' dugout. Now all I had to do was reach over and get Gaetti to sign my Homer Hankie. But he was in the on-deck circle. Great. It could be forever before he got back to the dugout.

One out, nobody on, my man stepped to the plate. Sensing that I didn't have much time left as a front-row trespasser, I prayed that he would make a quick out. The wind-up. The pitch. Gaetti swung and the ball went soaring into the rightfield stands.

A home run! A home run! As he trotted around the bases, I reached over the railing with pen and Hankie in hand. Then a very large hand grabbed my shoulder, and a very large security guard asked that I kindly return to my seat.

I never did get the autograph, but I got something better. Gary Gaetti hit a home run for me.

Stefanie Schmall

T he late 1920s and early 1930s was a colorful era, but we didn't think so at the time. The stock market crash and the start of the Great Depression translated into few, if any, jobs. Many of us turned to semipro baseball to earn a nickel or two. We played into autumn, traveling via a Model T Ford to neighboring town and cities. Six of us rode in the open car with bats, gloves, and, in fall, sweaters. Six gallons of gas for a dollar enabled us to go one hundred miles for twenty-five cents apiece. Collections taken at the game were usually the only source of revenue. Our share was sometimes five dollars. When the collection was slim, the ride home in the night air was longer and colder than usual.

Herb Nettleton

My sweetest baseball memory is of watching the 1986 World Series with my father—over the phone. He was in Boston, I was in New York, and we were both rooting for the Red Sox. He died shortly after that. I guess what I like most about baseball is that it reminds me of my dad.

Louise Godine

Y ears ago we were on a family vacation in New England. It had rained for days and we were hoping that the sun would finally make an appearance for the one day we had to spend seeing Boston. But our foul weather luck held firm, and as we took the "T" into the center city, the skies opened. My brothers and I were kind of nervous about wearing our orange Baltimore Orioles rain slickers into downtown Boston, the heart of Red Sox territory. We were the invading enemy; how would Bostonians react when they saw us coming decked out in full battle regalia? My father laughed at our worries, saying we had a responsibility to our team to hold our heads high even in the face of anticipated jeers and unfriendliness.

To our surprise, those slickers were the keys that unlocked for us the heart of Boston. Many people stopped to talk to us and share information about their city. We'd discuss our team's chances and their team's chances and the awful possibility that those hated men in pinstripes would slip in and steal the flag. We all agreed that if "our" team didn't win it, we hoped "theirs" would—anything but a pennant for the hated Yankees. Of course, people poked fun at us, but it was good-natured and full of the respect that true fans have for one another. For despite our deeply felt, separate loyalties, the thing that binds us and that we collectively celebrate is baseball itself.

Ann Batdorf

When I was ten my Uncle Gerald had an extra ticket for the fifth game of the 1956 World Series between the Dodgers and the Yankees at the stadium. Since I was the oldest nephew, and a certified baseball nut, I had claim to that extra ticket. But at the last minute Gerald's daughter said she wanted to go. Cousin Lois was a sixteen-year-old, boy-crazy, gum-chewing delinquent who didn't know the first thing about baseball.

Of course, Lois went to the game, the only professional baseball game she ever attended, and saw Don Larsen pitch the only perfect game in World Series history.

Jeffrey Laing

Mike Schacht

My first baseman's glove was once Lou Gehrig's. It had to have been. It was old; it looked like a big oven mitt; it had no manufacturer's tag and no autograph in the pocket. At first it was hard to handle. It had a thumb-and-pinky grip and it left the three other fingers with little room and little to do. But I could pick high throws on the stretch and it kept the ball snug in the upper reaches of the pocket.

With Ironman's mitt I caught throws from the infield with two hands. I pulled tosses out of the dirt with authority. It felt good against my thigh between pitches—like a companion by my side. It was Ironman's mitt, all right. It had to be.

Paul Turner

I was six years old and Mom had remarried. We took the train ten miles from Mattoon to Charleston so we kids could meet our new grandparents. I remember the day well—deep in winter, the Illinois countryside was covered with snow. We were as nervous as we were excited. We didn't know whether our new grandparents would love us or whether our new dad loved us, either.

Sometime during the day, I was in the kitchen with my new dad. His mother was cooking dinner on an old wood-burning stove. While rummaging for something in a drawer, she uncovered a ball glove. It turned out to be my new dad's old glove. It had been buried in that drawer since sometime before he went off to fight in World War II.

He handed it to me without saying a word. That one gesture made me feel loved and accepted by this man who was now my father. At that moment the glove was the single most important object in my life.

When anyone asks me who invented baseball, I say Charles E. Kerans did. It happened in Charleston, Illinois. There was snow on the ground that day.

F.N. Wright

I grew up glued to my brother's side. When we were young we used to go to the park with my dad and toss the ball around. I had a "girly" mitt, a smaller model with no player's signature on it. I was afraid of the ball hitting me, so I always (as Dad would tell me) "let the glove do the catching." Sometimes I would extend my arm so far out away from me that when the ball hit it, it would knock the glove off my hand. I can still picture the ball in my mitt on the ground and hear my dad yell, "Nice catch, nice catch!"

Jeanine Bucek

One Saturday morning at the end of the season, they held the Little League picnic. There was a contest to see who could throw a baseball the farthest. And I won! First prize was a new mitt. They told me that I could pick up my mitt when the awards ceremony started. I told them I had to go with my father and they said someone would hold it for me.

The next day I went to get my mitt. They said that because I wasn't at the awards ceremony they gave the prize to the second-place finisher.

Scott Reddin

It was the early spring of 1945 and I was a twelve-year-old growing up in Brooklyn. Because of the war, domestic travel restrictions were still in effect. The Dodgers were training up north, not far from New York, at Bear Mountain. Their manager, Leo Durocher, had complained in the press of the cold and dampness—and lack of equipment. My Uncle Larry said, "Bobby, why don't you offer the Dodgers your glove? Maybe they'll send us some free tickets." I sent Leo a letter.

A few days later a letter arrived addressed to me on Bear Mountain Inn stationery. It was dated April 5, 1945. In flowery, parochial school penmanship, it read:

Dear Robert,

*Thanks a lot for offering of glove, but at present every-
one has one. Will keep you in mind if someone should
need one. Again thanking you. Sincerely,*

Leo Durocher

When Leo died at eighty-six, I looked at the letter, now framed
and on my living room wall. For a moment I was twelve years old
again and the Dodgers were in Brooklyn.

Robert Gruber

When we were old enough to drive, those of us who regularly went to Reds games at Crosley Field had a scheme for parking free. A NO PARKING ANY TIME sign near the ballpark was loosely fastened to its pole. With a little effort we would remove the sign and hide it under the car while we were at the game. We would put it back on the pole each time when we left. The summer after we all graduated someone took the sign with him when he went off to college. Maybe it was a sign of things to come. I never got back to Crosley, and the Reds moved into Riverfront in 1970.

I still have the sign.

Mike Schacht

One morning when I was four years old, or maybe five, my brother George and I hauled glass jars of wheat into town. We put them in an old apricot box and pulled it along the sidewalk with a rope. As we were starting out, a jar broke. We set it aside.

That afternoon, our hauling finished, the two of us were playing baseball. As I made for home plate I stepped on a piece of the broken jar. Blood shot from my foot. My mother gathered me up, carried me into the kitchen, and put me on the table. She phoned the doctor, then stopped the bleeding with thumb pressure until he arrived to sew me up.

It's my first memory of playing baseball.

William Ahlschwede

When you step up to that plate, son,
I want you to have an idea.
Right now you got no idea; you're
Going up there empty-headed,
And you're back on the bench before
You know it.
Right now I'll even settle for
An idea that's not particularly good.
You can have the idea of
Your mama's fried chicken.
You can have the idea of
That blue tube top behind the dugout.
You can have the idea of
How much you hate my face.
Just have an idea.

Like if there's a man on third with less than two outs,
You could have the idea of
A long fly ball to get the runner home.
If a fast base runner is on first,
You could have the idea of
Taking a couple of pitches to give him a chance to steal.
If you've got a three-oh count,
Which I can't imagine you ever seeing
the way your head is now,
You could have the idea of
A little box in the strike zone, and
You're not swinging at anything out of the box.
See, what I'm trying to say to you, son, is
You've got to have an idea!

Gary Anderson

My Father was a pier superintendent.
He worked sixty or seventy hours a week
On the Brooklyn docks loading steel
Bound for San Francisco and the Golden Gate
Then under construction.

He died of a heart attack
On a beautiful spring day in 1941,
While sitting peacefully in his best Sunday clothes
In the backyard of our rented house on Glenwood Road.
While I was waiting for the ambulance,
Some kids I knew passed in a car
And asked me if I were going over to the school
To play baseball. Stupidly,
I told them I'd be over later.

John C. Pine

During the Depression, the people needed heroes, and the heroes came in two types. One was rich, sophisticated, carefree, wearing a dinner jacket and sipping a highball—the kind of Hollywood roles that William Powell, Fred Astaire, and Cary Grant played. These heroes lived lives unattainable by their fans. Actors Humphrey Bogart, James Cagney, Spencer Tracy, Henry Fonda, and James Stewart played the other kind of hero: poor, tough, honest, ordinary Joes, scrappy, wisecracking, living by their wits and making good by sheer ability and grit. This was the Gashouse Gang, and their brand of success was one to which their many fans could reasonably aspire.

Margery Kimbrough

Twenty-five years ago I sat between my father and my twin brother at my first night game. Yankees and Red Sox at Yankee Stadium. Bahnsen pitched and the Red Sox batter swung. The ball went almost straight up and began to drift slowly over the Yankee dugout. Soon it reached a point above us in the night sky and hung there, suspended on the spin that made its descent excruciatingly slow.

In the first row below the overhang of the second deck the three of us waited in reverent excitement as the forces of physics drew the ball down toward us. Frozen in my seat, I watched, my left hand squirming in my Spalding Richie Allen. I was certain the ball was heading straight for my brother. I knew it, I was sure. Straight to Mike, who had never been the outfielder I was. Dad shouted, "You got it, Pete! It's all yours, Pete!" I wanted Dad to be right, but I knew it was Mike's.

The ball fell silently into the first row of the deck above.

Peter J. Greenhill

Bill Chapman

W hen I start complaining about all the things that are wrong with baseball today, it occurs to me that I am really blaming baseball for all the things wrong with everything: higher prices, awful weather, poor quality, lousy service, drugs, long lines, blaring music, traffic jams, malls, crowds, etc, etc.

It's so easy to pile all my gripes on the players, the owners, the media, the agents and lawyers, artificial turf, the DH, the domes . . . There I go again!

Mike Schacht

I have always had a special appreciation for the players of the 1930s. I don't know if it's because they played during hard times or because they just loved the game and showed it. On the faces in my scrapbook pictures, I see an appreciation for the opportunity to play a game and earn a living in a time when other talented men were walking the sidewalks looking for work.

I don't see that look of appreciation in today's players.

Ray Medeiros

In the spring of 1930, in the midst of the Great Depression, no one had money for ball games. The Phillies, needing a cheering section in the City of Brotherly Love, extended that love to the ladies. We got to see the games free on Fridays. We trekked from Jay Cook Junior High at Thirteenth and Loudon streets to Baker Bowl at Broad and Lehigh, roughly four miles. We would swoon over the right fielder, Chuck Klein, a handsome bachelor. Dick Bartell and Jumbo Elliott were two of our favorites. Our high-pitched screams were a new experience for the players, and they responded. We were allowed to go on the field for autographs.

Margorie M. Muth

I recently had an opportunity to tag along with a television crew that was filming a piece on Marge Schott, the owner of the Cincinnati Reds. She was making a visit to a home of senior citizens in an Ohio retirement community. I've never seen anything quite like it. There must have been 150 senior Reds Rooters. They were all dressed in red. On cue they all greeted her with a chorus of "Take Me Out to the Ball Game." It was a lot like birthday parties I remember when I was little.

Wendy Schacht

Never mind, said Lindsay, a sausage-legged shortstop with gum in his cheek. All we needed was patience, he said, patience to wait for an outside fastball, high and tailing away—and wrists to smack it toward the slope beyond right field. Lindsay had that patience. One tied seventh inning, he got that pitch, spinning high, white and tailing away. He uncocked his elbows, snapped his wrists, chopped it toward the late season's orange sun. He lifted a drive toward the oak tree, the foul pole in right. It crackled through the branches, scattered leaves, fell among purple spikes of thistle on the hill. The outfielder just turned to watch it sail. In the bleachers his dad and mom, a sister, a young brother, three girls he knew from school, cheered as he stomped dust from the bases.

It has been twenty-five years since I wore elastic leggings, horsehide and leather snapped in my ears, since I was a second-sacker striking my glove and stirring a cleat in the dirt. Now I walk over stubble mowed for fear of fire, remembering this ground was thick with grass. The chalk has disappeared, base paths overgrown, the mound worn flat by winds and wet winters. The board-and-wire backstop remains, looming like a monument, and the carved sign that reads JOHN MCGINTY FIELD. The pasture that was right still rises toward the hill of mustard and thistle beneath the black oak that gathered in his drive.

When a clipboard hung from his bed, Lindsay gave up opening schoolbooks. He gave up talk of making the majors. Let me forget his shrunken body. Let me just smell mowed oats and feel a breeze from the bay. Let me dream bee's hum, a lizard's throat, a moon that rises beside Mount Hamilton. I'm dreaming dusk dissolves and deer come down to graze near the place where we watched a home run sail, where I saw Lindsay rounding third, where I waited for him to cross the plate before rushing forward to close him in my arms.

Gage McKinney

The hardest hit ball I ever saw was at Ebbets Field—a line drive to center by Eddie Mathews. It never rose more than waist high, striking the wall on one bounce before rebounding directly to Duke Snider, who hadn't moved from his position. Mathews rounded first and held, as though it had been just an ordinary single.

Daniel McGuire

I stopped at a thrift shop last weekend. I had a hunch that I might be lucky enough to find an old baseball glove, or a rare book or some other treasure. Sure enough, leaning against the wall behind the counter were two old baseball bats. I inquired about them only to learn that they were not for sale. They were for store security, for guarding the cash register.

Mike Schacht

Some people count sheep. I play baseball.

Every night just before I fall asleep, the Cleveland Indians and I play the New York Yankees, the team every Indians fan most wants to beat. Some people think the Indians are a second-rate team, and maybe they're right. Nonetheless, they are my team, a team that tugs at my heart and soul. And when they win, the victory is ever so sweet. They win every night just before I fall asleep. I make sure of it.

I set the lineup when my head hits the pillow. The game is always about the same. The Yankees lead as the game enters the bottom of the ninth. Last chance for the Indians. The crowd stomps its feet, hoping the rhythmic thunder will set off an Indian rally. I don't disappoint them. But I'm not after any ordinary victory. I want a dramatic win, one that will whip the crowd into a frenzy, something to talk about for weeks.

The Indians come from behind against the hated Yankees. What could be sweeter? Then, after a good night's work, I drift off to sleep.

Edward Allan Faine

My father wore steel-rimmed glasses, a suit and tie, and a hat. Always a hat. During the early 1950s he attended all my high school games—football, basketball, and baseball—so attired. That is the picture of him I carry in my mind more than any other.

During pregame warm-ups or time-outs, on deck waiting to bat, between pitches or on the bases, if I looked up he'd be there. Sometimes he would arrive late or have to leave early, but whenever the situation was crucial I knew he was there.

Now, as a father of three, I understand he must have been very proud watching me play in all those games. It's nice to think that maybe I gave him something back.

Mike Schacht

The first money I earned was for providing parking for Pirates games. I grew up in Pittsburgh, just up the hill from Forbes Field. On summer evenings I held a sign that read PARKING $1 and stood in front of our driveway yelling, "Parking! Parking! Park here for the ballgame!" I waved cars up the driveway and collected money until the driveway was full and I was $7 or $8 richer.

Around 11:30 the doorbell would start to ring, and my parents would open the door to Pirates fans wanting to know how they were supposed to get their cars out of the driveway and if they could use the bathroom. I slept blissfully through it all, the money tucked under my pillow.

Amy Benesch

In 1949 Bobby Sullivan was our town hero. In a week he'd be leaving for Florida. He'd signed with the Cincinnati Reds. Everyone in town was down at the high school, lined up to shag balls while his brothers took turns pitching batting practice.

I caught two on the fly, and took one home in my pocket.

Dick Brown

N.G. Schacht

I was the best hitter in our neighborhood. Nobody could throw one by me. I leaned way back with the bat and crouched low, like Lou Boudreau. I didn't copy him. I batted that way before I ever saw him play. I stayed in that crouch and hit real good, up to varsity ball in school. Then the coach told me I should bat standing straight up. Said I'd pull the ball more, hit it farther.

I did what he said. I stood straight up. Hit pretty good, but not as consistent as before. Plenty good enough to play high school ball, but I wasn't the best anymore. Maybe it was because the competition was better. But sometimes I think I might have made the big leagues if I'd stayed in that crouch.

Mark Soifer

I remember every error I've made.

I'm eleven. A huge pop fly soars out to right, and I shade over slowly. Three more steps and I settle under it, confident. The ball drops four feet to my right.

At twenty-one I'm in right again. The ball angles down the line, hard and low. A quick jump and it's mine, but my feet have other ideas. After I recover, there's little point in chasing it.

Six years later, in a game we need to win, a drive rockets to left. I've got plenty of time, jogging back step over step. Then I take a single, slower, more cautious step and the ball skips off the top of my glove.

Each morning as I walk to work I think about these moments. By the time I reach my office, I'm ready for whatever the day will bring.

Stephen S. Power

She played the romantic lead in many of my adolescent dreams. I was an intimidated fifteen-year-old and she was perfection. In the two high school classes we shared, our conversations were brief. *Can I borrow your eraser?*

I met her recently at our thirtieth high school reunion. Our conversation was again brief. I don't know whether it was age that had diminished her beauty and charm, or maturity that had dimmed my vision of her perfection. But whatever it was, I realized why I will never attend a baseball fantasy camp.

Robert Gruber

Love and baseball share a lot of common features—passion, loyalty, a fascination with special achievements and personalities, trust, hope, and a belief in destiny: a crazy notion that if things are meant to happen, they will. Love is something invented to keep you happy even during the times when your favorite baseball team stinks. Baseball works the same way, to keep you devoted to something other than waiting by the phone for Mr. or Ms. Right to call. The best combination? When both team and relationship are going well. Tennyson had it wrong. 'Tis better to have loved and *won.*

Jeanine Bucek

Here I sit in my bedroom, staring out the window and wondering why my mom is so mean. "Just wait till your father gets home," she said. "Then you tell him what you did to the new baseball glove he bought you." I just know my dad will understand and be able to explain it to Mom. Thank God he knows everything about baseball. *The little tricks of the trade make average players into good players.*

I had read or heard somewhere that Eddie Miller, the great fielding shortstop, cut the leather and padding out of the palm of his glove. This, he said, gave him better control of the ball when fielding it or shoveling it to the second baseman on double plays. If it was OK for Eddie Miller, it had to be OK for me. So when Dad gave me my first new glove, and because I dreamed of being a shortstop, I cut a hole in the palm with my dad's knife, pulled out the padding and pretended to be Eddie Miller (even though it really stung my hand to catch hard throws).

I bragged to my sister about what I had done and how much better a shortstop I would become. She tattled on me. Mom saw the glove and here I sit, waiting. But I know Dad will patch up the misunderstanding with Mom. I know he will explain to her the little tricks of the trade.

George Kelleher

Felix and I took our last walk today. I took him to the ball field down the street from my apartment where we often would go. I sat his cat hotel on home plate facing out toward the outfield and I told him some stuff.

A few moments later I took Felix to the vet to be put to sleep. We were partners for eleven years. Although it was the most difficult decision that I have ever had to make, I couldn't prolong his agony any longer.

For the past several summers I have traveled quite a bit photographing baseball. It bothered me to be away from him for more than a week or two at a time, and I planned my trips accordingly. After my returns his response was always the same. There were several moments of indifference, then a sharp bite on my hand and all was forgiven. I understood. One of my last comments to him was that we wouldn't get to watch the World Series together.

A few weeks later I went back to the ball field. In the brief time since our last walk, a tractor had begun to dig up the field. I looked at the circular lines that it had created, which seemed to swirl from home plate, and I thought: Home plate is really the center of it all and everything begins there. Most importantly life, but sometimes death.

Bill Chapman

I became a baseball fan in 1977. My father was watching the American League playoffs on TV, and he asked me to watch with him. I really wasn't interested because baseball seemed like a dumb game to me. I watched anyway.

The Yankees were up. Bucky Dent came to the plate. I fell in love. I was thirteen, he was cute and his name was Bucky. My family had been calling me Bucky for years because of my buck teeth. Suddenly the nickname I had always hated didn't seem so bad.

A week after that playoff game, an 8 × 10 autographed picture came in the mail. It said, "To Bucky—Love Always, Bucky Dent." I never missed a Yankee game after that. Thanks for making me watch the game, Dad.

Stefanie Schmall

D orothy McLaughlin was tall at twelve, with deep red hair razored short, round freckled cheeks, and broad shoulders. She played for the rival Dodgers in my Little League. I remember one game she struck me out, then two innings later switched to second and threw me out. She had three hits too, I think.

I had lots of little crushes in grammar school, weeklong loves for cute girls in small white sneakers and blonde ponytails. My crush on Dorothy . . . that was the only one that felt like something real.

Stephen S. Power

Not much catches my eye,
except I noticed
the lopsided valentine stuck
to the upstairs window
across the way, its Crayola red
brilliance shocking
as the blinding sun
that July Saturday I galloped
under the high fly to left field,
my glove a shovel
and the moms and dads
with me. "You got it!"
"You got it!" Me, ready to grab
the white pill dropping,

dropping, black
against the blood sun
and my heart in my mouth
until I missed the ball
and the stands broke
into a silence where I heard
my heart break and my love
for the game died
except for odd days
when the glass catches
the sun like the heart
in the window across the way
grabs my eye.

Barbara M. Simon

My father is eighty-three years old. During the long winter he spends most of his days just sleeping. There is no stimulation in his life. Then spring training comes, and he is alive! During the baseball season, right up through the World Series, he reads the sports pages, watches games on television, listens to them on radio, and constantly talks baseball. It is his only interest, the only thing that keeps him going. Then fall, and winter, and the cycle begins again.

Reba Shimansky

The uptown Number 4 train is packed with Yankee fans, all generally in high spirits, yakking it up as our sardine-can-on-wheels rumbles toward Yankee Stadium. "Look," says a guy standing near me, grinning and pointing out the window. In turn, I have to smile back at him, because even without looking I know why he is beaming; he's just seen that wonderful opening in the stadium where you get a brief and tantalizing glimpse of the playing field. I get a kick out of watching someone else react to that first sight of green grass and diamond.

Diane Lesniewski

The ball made a small sound as it hit.
I felt something loosen
in my hand. Red dust
rose from the field as you ran
toward me.

Terri Richburg

"Campy was the hardest man I ever met,"
Kahn the sportswriter said.

Campy, the guinea-nigger-halfbreed,
Kneeling in a Germantown sandlot
With bruised ribs and a ball in his glove.

Campy rising at 1 A.M. to deliver milk
And two blocks worth of papers.
Campy who had three grown men pull up

In a white Caddy convertible,
Pay his momma three times
daddy's weekly wage to let him

Catch games on the weekends.
Campy who quit school at fifteen. Spent ten
years squatting in the Negro leagues,

Birmingham to Harlem. Spent ten winters
In the Latin Leagues—Mexico,
Puerto Rico, Venezuela—making the year

A hard and dusty perpetual summer.
Campy who got the call from Mr. Rickey
To be number four and join Robinson at Ebbets.

Campy who slept across town
While the rest laughed it up
And danced a block from the stadium.

Campy who got MVP in '51, '53 and '55.
Campy who had mitts so sore he couldn't
Lift the trophy. Who sat upside-down

In an icy car in a Long Island ditch
Thinking how he couldn't feel his legs.
Who sat upstairs, looking out the window,

While his wife made love to another man
In the front seat of a Pontiac.
And Campy who grew old remembering

A September afternoon. And that sound.
And how the ball rose steadily
Just inside the third base line

And how he thought,
"Jesus, sweet Lord Jesus, oh it's good to be alive."

Jerry Wemple

Not how much talent have I, but how much *will* to use the talent that I have. That is the main question.

W.C. Gannett

The first batter steps to the plate and the home crowd responds: Yells of encouragement to the field, screams at the batter and pounding on the bleachers. We are caught up in the magic of the game.

I look across the field and my eyes settle on the shortstop, as they always have. His tall, lean body is set, crouched low, glove hand extended, eyes intent on the batter.

I blink and in my mind I see that body much younger, sitting in a small boat trolling along the lake shore, those same eyes intent on a fishing line.

With a loud crack, metal and ball collide and bring me back to the game. The ball skims across the infield, kicking up dust. The shortstop, in one smooth motion, gloves it and fires to first.

The moment becomes slow motion. I smile, and as I watch the ball flatten in midair I hear the sound of waves against a shore. He has thrown a flat, smooth rock with all his might to skim across the lake. "Four, five, six, seven . . . that's a record," he says, squinting up at me, the sun in his face, sand clinging to his wet legs and a ring of white showing a tan line where his bathing suit has dropped below his belly.

"You're out!" calls the ump, and I return to the game to watch my shortstop punch the sky.

Joyce Arnold

Bleachered behind the lace curtains
of my third floor window,
I saw down the diamond church courtyard,
walled garden cloister closed
to the rest of teeming Chicago.

Studs Terkel and Mike Royko
were not invited there
to Wood Street
on the South Side
of an early '60s spring.

No hot dogs, fans
or bleacher bums to bellow boos.
Just Mom and me up there
in the cheap seats.
We watched them
mark off base lines,
choose up sides.

Holy habited nuns
tied back headgear,
hitched up their heavy skirts

to exposed black stockinged legs
and sneakered feet.

Veils flew
curls; blonde, gray, red
shook loose.
Sweat broke,
bats cracked bases run
The Sisters of Mercy
showed none.
One big nun
with feet to match
always wore plaid sneakers,
red.

Marked beacon
in a sea of black and white,
she slid Home
Run scored!
A sign of things to come.

Pat Bartolo

It was mostly mud. Here and there a few patches of brown grass poked through, hoping that the snow had paid its last visit of the year. The backstop was pretty much the way I remembered it; the chain link was still sturdy enough to hang a bat from. The school itself was all boarded up.

I walked toward third, noticing that the path from second was rutted with a nasty gash. No thief on his best day could have slid so long and so deep. Most likely some kid on a motorbike, I figured. Some kid who didn't appreciate the game.

The outfield, though, was in much better condition. In most spots, the grass was healthy and green. A few ponds were still in evidence, but the thaw was about over now, and soon the spring sun would steam away the pools and bake over the mud—the grass would cover the infield and outfield with a thick, emerald matte—and the diamond would be reborn, ready for another season.

David Blanchard

Bill Chapman

I saw Ebbets Field for the first and last time on a sunny November day in 1959, two years after Walter O'Malley removed the Brooklyn Dodgers to Los Angeles and only months before it fell under the wrecker's ball. During one of my aimless perambulations in pursuit of pictures, I found myself in a neighborhood which seemed to have been not so much allowed to run down as evacuated. There, amid unoccupied frame houses, a flowering of weathered advertising signs and boarded-up refreshment stands, was, becalmed, forgotten but not gone, Ebbets Field. The only sound was the flapping of a nearby awning bearing the legend RED HOTS. I felt like a gringo tourist in the Yucatan who had stumbled onto a Mayan temple. Walking around to Bedford Avenue, where, the world knew, home runs had once rained, I heard a familiar sound. Carried on the wind were ghostly cheers from the disenfranchised fans of Flatbush for Robinson, Reese, Furillo, and all the departed summer boys. The cheering did not abate but went on and on until, turning the corner onto Montgomery Avenue, I could no longer hear it.

Robert Weaver

V ivid memories of an autograph seeker:

Jackie Robinson, after a game, in the Ebbets Field rotunda, a big man with big shoulders and big hands and rippling muscles. He said, *This scorecard looks ten years old.* Bobo Newsom, in a suit, sitting alone at the bar in the cocktail lounge of the New Yorker Hotel on 34th Street. My friends and I afraid to walk in. He said, *Come on in, kid, you won't get kicked out.* Charley "Red" Barrett, soaked with sweat, his freckled face still red, in the St. Louis bullpen at Ebbets Field after beating the Dodgers in the first game of a Sunday doubleheader. He said, *Kid, it's a pleasure and I'm feeling great.* Mel Ott, carrying a carton of Chesterfields into the elevator at the New Yorker Hotel. He said, *Not today, not today, sonny.* Jack "Lucky" Lohrke, that great arm from third base, riding the subway uptown to the Polo Grounds. He said, *As many as you want . . . You know who I am, don't you?*

William Lucano

In 1948 I attended my first major league game; my dad took me to old Shibe Park in Philadelphia to see the Phillies play. From that point on I was an ardent Phillies fan. Two seasons later, my "Whiz Kids" won the National League pennant, and the awesome Yankees, with Joe DiMaggio in the twilight of his marvelous career, notched yet another American League title.

In the first game of the World Series the New Yorkers prevailed 1–0. In the second game, after nine tense innings, the teams were tied at one. DiMaggio had been hitless in his first eight at-bats in the series. In the tenth inning, however, he hit a towering drive to the rooftop of the double-decked left-field stands at Shibe Park, winning the game and crushing my hopes. As I listened to the game on radio in my sixth-grade classroom, it seemed my life had been changed forever by a Joe DiMaggio home run.

The Yankees, of course, finished the four-game sweep at Yankee Stadium. But for all intents and purposes, the series ended with that one majestic, heartbreaking swing of the bat by the great DiMaggio.

Andy Jurinko

He mows grass and works in the cafeteria,
Back on the diamond only in dreams.
And when one of his fifteen-cent cards resurfaces
    in the grubby hands of a wide-eyed student,
The monotony of his life is
    Broken.
But just for a fleeting second.

And in that instant,
    he assumes the once-familiar autograph stance.
He is back to that one glorious September
When pens and cards were handed to him every day.
He can see himself there, younger,
Maybe not fully appreciating the glory of it all
But still knowing it was special.

And never dreaming it would end.

James Kaufman

I never knew my grandfather, but one of my favorite stories about him is his reported ability to listen simultaneously to separate ball games on the radio—a Milwaukee Braves game and a Washington Senators game—and be fully aware of the scores and stats of each. When he later purchased a television, I am told, he would watch one game and listen to two others on his portable radios.

Sometimes when I'm watching a game or leafing through my grandfather's collection of World Series newspaper clippings, I can see him sitting in his chair enjoying it all.

Todd Womack

My grandfather gave me his scrapbook, and I memorized it.

In 1938, he was voted Most Valuable Player for Shickshinny in the TriCounty League. The yellowed articles all referred to him as "the hard-hitting outfielder." They played teams from neighboring coal mining towns: Catawissa, Benton, Nescopek. As the team's leading hitter with a .361 average, he won a $5 award from Chick's Auto in Berwick. At the end of the season, he received his unconditional release and moved to Baltimore to raise a family with his new bride, the Bloomsburg State College Beauty Queen.

I remember we used to listen to Oriole games on a black radio, a Zenith. His arms were around mine the first time I made contact with a whiffle ball. "Swing level. Hit line drives," he said.

I was ten years old when we won the Baltimore County championship. The score was 18–7. I got a couple of hits in the game and he pressed a $5 bill in my hand afterward. He told everyone in his neighborhood about the game. He made me feel like the best ballplayer in the world.

I can still see him in his lawn chair down the third base line. He seemed like my real father back then.

Dean Smith

I wish I'd had this network of baseball friends thirty years ago when many of my special friends were still around. There's a lot of truth in the saying, "When an old-timer dies, it's like a library burns down." We don't just lose our memories of the time shared with them, we lose *their* memories, too.

Ray Medeiros

Old man squeezes
a pockmarked rubber ball,
his right arm circles back,
forward over his head toward
a barn wall no longer there

Edward J. Rielly

Lakeland, Florida, is the Citrus Center of the World. It is also the spring training camp of the Detroit Tigers. In 1961, before semester break during my freshman year at Florida Southern College in Lakeland, all freshman women were summoned for a meeting with Miss Hattie Eicholtz, dean of women.

Dean Eicholtz's pronouncement to her assembled subjects was to alert us to the dangers of playing with Tigers. To paraphrase: Some men are, ahem, unscrupulous; they'll prey upon the innocence of young ladies and take advantage of them. They might even remove their wedding bands so that we would think them single. We were not, under any circumstance, to entertain professional ballplayers either on or off campus without written permission from our parents.

Years later, when I was a reporter for the daily newspaper in Lakeland, I learned that a similar warning was issued to Tigers players [about us].

Sallie Batson

Day five of sobriety and still riding high atop
the wagon, sipping cool waters every so often,
knowing from past how damn easy it is to say
"screw it," hop in the take-out store, grab an
icy sixer and flee,

recalling the "hey Zeus" buzz and freedom
of bumping over old two-wheel dirt trails with
fresh baroodies in one hand, bitter black cigar
smoldering, wind blowing dust all over,

now limping past pink neon shadows,
"cold beer to go" signs with tired nonchalance of
Don Larsen walking to the pitcher's mound,
big World Series game, knowing it has to be
"three up and three down" for the rest of
his life.

T. Kilgore Splake

Old ballplayers should be skinned and turned into gloves.

Eric Rolfe Greenberg

He pitches—"So, do you like baseball?"

And she crushes it—"You have to enroll me in the big deal about baseball. For me, it's like, so what?"

Mike Schacht

Mike Schacht

The key to being a good baseball conversationalist is to be a good listener.

My problem is that when I meet someone who knows and likes baseball as much as I do, I start talking faster than I can think. I want to show off how much I know. I get overexcited and sometimes even get my facts wrong. I try to anticipate what they will say and interrupt with answers before they can finish. It's terrible. It's embarrassing. Everybody gets frustrated or angry, or both.

Over the years I've gotten a little bit better, but I still think I have a problem. "In any adult," the late Bart Giamatti once said, "will always lurk a child."

Mike Schacht

At age two, while watching a game on the tube, my daughter found her first baseball hero. The 1979 Mets were playing Montreal, and Doug Flynn, the Mets second baseman, hit a ball as hard as he had ever hit one, on a line, directly over the head of the Montreal left fielder, Warren Cromartie. Cromartie raced back, nearly keeping time with the ball, and both the ball and Cromartie hit the wall at the same instant.

The ball rebounded. Cromartie did not. He crumbled to the ground, and stayed there.

This caught Elinor's attention. But what made a far deeper impression was the manner in which, over the next seven minutes, Cromartie ran into the wall again and again and again—in slow motion, in stop action, from this angle and from that. And crumbled to the ground every time.

For the next week, Elinor ran around the apartment, crashing into walls and falling to the floor, gleefully announcing, "I'm Warren Cromartie! I'm Warren Cromartie!"

Eric Rolfe Greenberg

My dad walked dreamy-eyed from chore to chore
toiling from sun to moon.
I walked beside him wondering where he was,
sought phrases that might reach into
his silence,
make him talk to me.

One afternoon he joined our game of scrub
in the shadowed cool
behind the shed.

He pitched with easy grace
relaxed and present in the game.
I stood at bat.
The ball came hard.
I checked my swing.

The ball smashed into my face
numb at first
until heat spread, stinging, throbbing.
I felt lips thicken, press against my teeth.

He loped toward me
game forgotten as he held me
brushed the hair out of my eyes
gingerly touched my cheek.
"I didn't mean to."
The game was over.

I'm still not sure
if I didn't step into the ball.

Carol Thornton

W hat I really miss about baseball is the surety there will be a next season, so the machinations and deals of the winter mean something. Maybe thinking of baseball gets me through the winter better than the games do in summer.

Luke Salisbury

My parents were German immigrants and cared nothing for baseball. I grew up feeling much the same way.

Years later I moved to New York and met my husband, who insisted I watch his beloved Yankees with him. In no time I became a devoted fan, too. One night as we were watching *Pride of the Yankees,* a light bulb clicked on in my head. My parents had mentioned many times, with pride, that my grandfather's cousin, Jacob Ruppert, had been the owner of a famous New York brewery. The same Jacob Ruppert was the owner of the Yankees in the days of Ruth, Gehrig, and DiMaggio. Holy Cow!—they didn't think the Yankees were even worth mentioning.

Ivy Fischer Stone

In the summer of my twelfth year I harassed my mother into calling Ty Cobb to ask if she could bring me by to meet him. I had learned that he lived ten or fifteen miles from us. At first Mom said no. We had lived in Georgia for many years before our move to California and she was well acquainted with his reputation. "He's not a nice man," she told me. But I persisted, and finally she called.

"Of course," he said. "When can you be here?"

The next morning we made the drive from Los Altos up the peninsula to Atherton, where he lived. He showed me his baseball mementoes, answered all my questions, and posed for photos I took with my Brownie.

"Bring him back," he told my mother.

A few weeks later she did, and left me there while she and a friend went shopping. We talked some more, played catch, ate lunch. Then Mom returned.

"Bring him again," he said, but it never happened. My school and my mother's job prevented it, but I believed I would visit him again someday. I figured he'd be in Atherton forever.

I never went back. Years later, I read of his death.

Brent Kelley

N. G. Schacht

I found the glove soaking wet and deserted at the playground, half hidden in the grass behind the backstop. Nobody claimed it, so I took it. Finders keepers. I slipped it on my hand, pounded my right fist in it, and thought, "Pretty good."

The first time I used it, in a neighborhood game three days later, after it had dried stiff and unyielding, I went to take a throw at second from Jackie Spangler. The baseball sailed over the top of the glove and crashed into my nose. There was a sudden flurry of guys around me, everyone trying to stop the bleeding with grimy handkerchiefs and wads of grass.

Big Roy Wells said the glove was cursed—*Why do you think you even found the damn thing, you dummy?*—and opinion was fairly well split between Roy's and the notion that I just wasn't paying attention. Jackie examined the swollen and wobbly cartilage of my nose, said he was sorry and to hold the glove higher next time. Tom Rike sided with Roy and said to dump the glove.

I kept it. Through adolescence, high school and college, young adulthood and playing catch with my kids, I wore that mitt. There were errors and desperate stabs, but hardly cursed catastrophes. A few years ago, its pocket worn wafer thin, laces popped and broken, little pieces of leather flaking off, I put it away. Sometimes my sons see it in the basement, slip it on a hand and pound a fist in it. They don't say, "Pretty good." They say, "You need a new glove, Dad." *No, I don't.*

Kevin Grace

As it smashed into his glove
the boy fell backward.

He had caught it.
It had caught him.

Anthony DeGregorio

I listen late at night. My wife is asleep. My son moves in his crib as if the Red Sox are troubling his sleep. Millions of people are listening to baseball.

The night belongs to us.

Luke Salisbury

Wₑ did all the same things. Of course, I thought I did most things better than he did. We competed in everything. I was bigger. He was tougher. (Besides my brother, he was the only one who ever gave me a bloody nose.) We both collected baseball cards. I went to Crosley Field more than he did, but he traveled more than I did. He had a postcard collection. I started one. I sent away for college football programs. So did he. We built two tree houses together, one in his yard, one in mine. We biked everywhere together (he had a better bike). We went to different schools. We had different careers. He stayed. I moved away. We lost touch with one another.

The other day I found a picture of our grade school baseball team. We were together, holding up a sign (that I made) that said 1946 CHAMPS. I was pitcher and he was catcher. I was ten years old and he was my best friend.

Mike Schacht

I made my baseball debut
on Sister Marie Ann's eighth grade team.
Wally Fallon had the mumps
I played right field by default.
As game time approached
fear and joy made my stomach
feel like sauerkraut.
I ran out on the field, praying . . .
Lord, please don't send a fly ball my way.

I stood, baseball cap squared
body poised, glove at the ready.
The image was strong
but the knees were jello.
The Lord was good until the last inning

Game tied . . . bases loaded,
the dreaded horsehide sailed my way.

My eyes locked on the ball,
the brain computed velocity, trajectory.
I desperately ran
to the point of interception.
I stopped, turned, put up my glove,
the ball hit . . . ten feet behind me!

Later, Sister said . . .
"Well, at least
you're a good reader."

George Monagan

Jim Leyritz, my favorite player, stepped in to bat with his unique stance. There was a loud *crack*. I looked up to watch the ball rocketing into the sky, but in the brilliant sun I saw only a small black dot, and it was falling toward me. I reached up with my glove and a split second later the ball slammed into it, then popped out and bounced away. But I snagged it, as if I was playing a game of catch.

Three months later the Yanks were back in town. I took my baseball out to the stadium and caught up to Leyritz. I told him how I had caught it, and he smiled and said, "Oh yeah?" Then he signed it for me.

Many players scoff at signing autographs or talking to their fans. It made this eight-year-old happy to know that some, like Jim Leyritz, actually care for their fans.

Eric A. Christensen

My dad spent one full summer teaching Norman Hunt to throw a ball in our chain-linked backyard. My brother and I never questioned it, never questioned the time without him. We knew Norman didn't have a dad, and we knew he would never learn to throw without *our* dad. And we went down to the fields, my brother and me, to cheer him on during every one of his games.

Just recently my father told me of a story about Norman in the *Mineola American,* that he had just graduated from the Massachusetts Institute of Technology. Never *could* throw a ball.

Patricia Baker

The *crack* shattered the air. The ball screamed off the bat on a line, a low, solid, line drive that shot past the infielders and past the outfielders before they could take more than half a step.

He remembered the sheer electric thrill of it, the exquisitely sweet shock wave that rippled from his hands up his arms into his chest down his legs and right out through his toes.

Don Frankel

I was sitting on the first-base side of the upper deck at Shea Stadium when a Gooden fastball was hit to deep right field by Barry Larkin. Keith Miller drifted back and picked the ball out of the air and in one fluid motion hurled it toward third. The runner, tagged and ready at second, had to hold.

It was not the most glamorous or dramatic play in baseball; not one made by a legend, or even an everyday player. It was just a good catch followed by a good throw. I don't know why, but I stood and cheered Miller's play so loud that the fans sitting around me turned and seemed to wonder whether I was watching a different game.

Andy Blitz

T he night was cool, the season was spring, and I don't remember who played the Mets that night. At the end of the game I chose to remain in my seat. Within minutes the stands had cleared, and the orange seats glowed unnaturally in the flourescent lights. The sweepers on the field made circles around the bases, erasing all the plays now a part of baseball history. Policemen stood hunchbacked in twos and threes, arms crossed in front of blue shirts, talking.

How quiet it was. Within minutes the stands no longer reverberated with catcalls, game announcements, the seventh-inning stretch, the whistles, the boos, the "Darryl!" cheers, the jets overhead. It was just me.

When an orange-suited sweeper asked me to leave, I looked at him as though he were crazy. "This is so beautiful," I said. "You get to see this every night?"

"Yeah," he answered. "That's why I want to go home."

Bronwen Latimer

As a young boy, I was introduced to baseball by radio. It was when the Tigers and Cubs met in the 1945 World Series. That series proved to be the one baseball experience I shared with my father. The next spring he died.

My mother and I moved across the Michigan border to the little town of Lyons, Ohio. I spent my summer afternoons in the back room of our small, red house, listening to Tiger broadcaster Harry Heilmann. Harry became my teacher and summer companion, and he created a new world for me. A former player, he had known them all: the Babe, Cobb, Speaker, Cochrane, Greenberg, the Deans, Gehrig. I listened, and Harry weaved his fascinating tales.

In the summer of 1950 I visited my cousin in Chicago, and he took me to Comiskey Park to see my first major league game. From our center field seats I squinted to find home plate and get my bearings. I saw balls pitched and then soar into the air in strange arcs. I heard the crowd cheer in a muted tone. I felt a strange silence. Then I realized—no Harry.

Herschel Engebretson

I first became aware of baseball when I was three or four, lying on the floor of our living room. My father sat in his armchair watching a baseball game on television. I wanted to stay with my dad and do what he was doing, so I kept watching. It was an exercise in endurance because I didn't understand anything—just a green picture with a bunch of men in white running around, stopping and starting.

But I stayed until it was over. And the next time my dad watched a ball game, I watched with him. And the next time and the next. And gradually he started to explain, so I could understand, what all those men in white were doing and why. That green picture gradually came into sharper focus, the men in white became "my team," and I was hooked.

Ann Batdorf

As a boy I worshipped the Brooklyn Dodgers. For years I relived every pitch Red Barber called in the final game of the 1955 World Series in which Johnny Podres defeated the hated Yankees 2–0. Podres was a god.

Eleven years after that series, I was an eighteen-year-old sitting on the bench for the Troy Haymakers in the Capital District Amateur League. Coach Ginerski would fill out his roster with the best prospects from the area high school and American Legion teams. I was a decent fielder and could hold my own against even the best area pitching. In a season-ending tournament we faced a potbellied lefty who didn't look like he could break a pane of glass. We got hopelessly behind and I begged the coach to let me take my licks against this old-timer. I pinch hit in the seventh inning and couldn't even get a loud foul ball off this over-the-hiller. I was cursing and taking a riding from the older players when Coach Ginerski came over.

"Son, you now have something to tell your grandchildren," he said. "You just struck out against a former major leaguer. Ever hear of Johnny Podres?"

Jeffrey Laing

"How come you know so much about baseball?" I'm asked that question by a lot of guys, and every time it makes me laugh. Why shouldn't a woman know about baseball? Women have eyes, we have hearts and brains, we can see beauty. Sometimes we're taught it by our mothers or fathers, or sisters or brothers, or friends; sometimes we stumble over it ourselves by accident. That's what happened to me. My parents weren't fans, but when I found baseball at the age of eleven, it wasn't long before I'd infected them with my passion.

Years later, a lot of other aspects of life had intruded and baseball had faded into the background. My cap and glove were in a closet somewhere, stuffed in a box with other relics. But becoming a fan is something that can't be undone. We can drift away from the game for a hundred different reasons, but there's always a piece of us that once belonged to baseball. Someday we're likely to fall in love with the game all over again.

My old cap is a little tight, but my hand fits the glove better than it used to.

Heather Henderson

My dream is to find my future husband sitting in the stands at Yankee Stadium. "Go where the men are," singles guides say. For me that means a trip to my favorite place. I feel cheated if I sit beside a couple, or next to Mom, Dad, and the kids.

Once I almost married a man who didn't like baseball. "Please take me to a game, Russell," I begged. He refused. He didn't like any sports, except auto racing.

At the first game I ever attended at Fenway Park I sat next to a guy named Eric and his friend Larry. It was May 8, Eric's birthday. We talked during most of the game. He had the kindest eyes I've ever seen. He was one of the nicest men I've ever met. When the game ended, he and his friend were lost in the crowd.

I'm still going to the stadium, hoping for a little miracle—to meet someone special who can appreciate me and baseball, in that order. Then we can raise a brood of Yankee fans, and we can all watch the games together. Like I watched with my parents.

Diane Lesniewski

W e had no special reverence for baseball cards in my neighborhood. We bought them, a few packs at a time, and stuffed all the pink rectangles of gum into our mouths at once. Jaws straining, we thumbed through the cards in search of Yankees—Mantle or Maris or Ford—finding instead two or three Johnny Logans. The cards would go into a drawer or onto a shelf in the garage or even into the trash.

Seeking rescue from the boredom of an August afternoon, we grabbed a few cards and clipped them with clothespins to the spokes of our bicycles, piercing the thick heat with the flapping roar of our "motors." Or we fetched Dad's magnifying glass and sat on the curb under the broiling sun, burning holes into Johnny Logan's eyes.

John Simonson

Barnstorming

Most of us started playing as kids.
Back then, if you didn't play baseball,
you were a sissy. Mornings, we'd mow
a few lawns, then take in a cowboy matinee.
Afterwards, we'd kick up dust till dark,
sometimes after. If the ball busted,
we'd sew it back up. Didn't count
innings, we just played for hours.

We'd ride to the next town
in an old hay truck. A guy
at the game took up a collection
in a hat. After his take,
we'd have about 25 cents left
to buy a bottle of bellywash.

When I played for the Bobcats,

the owners moved us up North.

A dozen men, traveling in two cars:

a seven-passenger Buick and a Ford

with a rumble seat. On the way

to New York, it rained cats and dogs.

We had to take the equipment

off the roof, lay it across our laps.

The owners put us up at the Theresa.

One morning, one of the players

leaned out the window, caught

the hotel manager selling our cars

to pay for the rooms. That

was the end of the team.

Carole Boston Weatherford

I had strong feelings when I learned last year that Jim Palmer was thinking of attempting a comeback, hoping to become the only Hall of Fame inductee to return to the game as an active player. Palmer's prime, his golden years, coincided with my childhood and adolescence, when baseball and the fortunes of the Baltimore Orioles were everything that was important in my life. A vivid memory has me sitting with my best friend in the third seat of the family station wagon, back when they still made them facing backward, stopping at a red light, and watching in disbelief as Palmer pulled up behind us in his sportscar. It was too amazing. He laughed behind his sun visor, giving us the thumbs-up sign as we waved frantically. We were on Cloud Nine for the rest of the day.

I wanted Palmer's comeback to succeed, because if he could turn back the clock, then so could I. If I could sit in the stands on a warm, bright afternoon and watch Number 22 stride to the mound and start that familiar, graceful motion, it seemed possible that I could escape the choices and stresses of adulthood and return to those clear, magic days.

Ann Batdorf

Mike Schacht

Once when I was a young girl growing up in Florida I was playing baseball with my father and some neighborhood kids. I was in the outfield, the ball was hit to me, I grabbed it and with much enthusiasm threw it toward first base. It didn't make it. The runner was safe and much to my dismay I heard my father screaming, "You throw the ball just like a girl!" To which I responded, "I *am* a girl!" I was so angry the next time the ball came to me I threw it with all my might at my father. I was mortified when, wouldn't you know, the ball hit him in the crotch.

Fran Peters

I remember attending the 1939 New York World's Fair. A group of visitors were listening to a Dodger game on the radio. I heard them start to cheer, and joined in. When they saw I was a Dodger fan, too, I was immediately welcomed into their group and invited to share in the celebration. Being female might have made a difference, too. Girls weren't supposed to know anything about baseball, and I knew a lot, thanks to the radio and Red Barber.

For a shy thirteen-year-old with a lot of imagined problems, rooting for a baseball team was a way to become part of a group. If you've got a team to root for, you never have to be alone.

Alice Lee

I doubt the Northmont Amateur Baseball League of Englewood, Ohio, has kept records of this sort, so I'll set the facts straight. It was a triple play.

The Farmer's State Bank team I played on when I was ten was mediocre at best. We lost most of our games that season. I was the first baseman, but I was banished to center field for this particular game (probably for being a smart aleck—the coach said I read too much). We were playing Valley Tool & Die. It was the bottom of the fourth and they had runners on first and second with no outs.

I was playing a shallow center to be closer to my friends, the infielders, when the batter lifted a soft fly behind second. The runners took off and so did I, catching the ball chest high on the run and stepping on second base. I flipped the ball to our surprised first baseman, trotted in to our bench and sat down.

The players were all still on the field. I shouted to the umpire, "Hey, the inning's over." Those are the facts.

Kevin Grace

Trust me, the average baseball fan in L.A. doesn't know what the seventh-inning stretch is. No matter how exciting a game is, L.A. fans would rather beat the traffic than watch to the end.

It makes no sense. A mass exodus begins just before the start of the seventh inning. Everyone ends up stuck in a massive parking-lot traffic jam, listening to the balance of the game on car radios.

F.N. Wright

I enjoy doing something good and meeting a lot of people. I want to be either a baseball announcer or work in baseball public relations, so this is my start: I work for the Reading Phillies of the Class AA Eastern League. I am known as "The Rubbish Ranger." I dress up in work outfit, team baseball hat, and Lone Ranger mask. My job is to pick up the trash from the fans in the stands all season. I sign, on average, a dozen autographs a night.

Alen Beljin

New York Divorce

Relaxing with his son   Relaxing with her son
watching the Mets,   watching the Yankees,
sharing the good times   sharing the good times
together.   together.
The court gave him   The court gave her
the best home dates   the best home dates
to root for their team   to root for their team

                   as a family

                              Robert L. Harrison

T hough I'd never seen a baseball field, I could paint a picture just from listening to his radio voice. I felt the impact, timing, texture, the geometric shape of every play, memorized the batting orders and every player's name. I knew the weight, mass, the speed of every ball; shifted the thick, wet wad tucked in the batter's cheek, and challenged the umpire's call. I saw the windup, stretch, delivery, felt the viscosity of stadium heat; heard a bat fan the breeze after a slow sweet curve dropped in at the knees.

Alice Lee

My eight-year-old son Kenny came to bat shortly after I had been pressed into serving as an emergency umpire at one of his Little League games. Standing behind the pitcher I watched him foul off two pitches. The next pitch was a perfect strike down the middle. Kenny didn't move.

"Strike three!" I called. "Yer out!" Our eyes met. I'll never forget the look on his face.

Recently he told me, "Dad, it took me almost twenty years to understand. It's OK. You did the right thing."

Louis W. Doroshow

Today's Memorial Day game is a family
affair—anything over the rosebushes
down the left field line, anything
on the roof down the right field line
or past the yellow Cougar to center
is out of here, touch 'em all.
Anything into the ornamental waterfall
or lost in the hedge is two bases.
Ground rules over. Play ball!

Bill Cowee

Today I'm in my yard,
again upon the mound,
now pitching to my little boy,
whose swing can't get around.

And *I* want him to hit;
I strive to serve it fat.
But try as very best he can,
he cannot wield the bat.

Time was, long years ago,
I would've killed for this—
to watch the batters lunge and flail
and hack and grunt and miss.

Though now I'm in command,
this isn't any thrill.
I know that all sons rout their dads,
and that mine someday will.

G.J. Searles

Bill Farrell

When our friends and relatives reminisce about our wedding, they say that the ceremony was very spiritual, the flower girls' dresses were exquisite, and the chocolate cake with tiers of pink icing flowers was a work of art. Then they start singing "Take Me Out to the Ballgame."

That's because the party my husband threw at the Yankees-Mariners game the day before nearly overshadowed the main event. We had the Billy Martin Suite, an open bar, six-foot hero sandwiches, unlimited chili dogs, our name up in lights on the message board, perfect weather, and a personal congratulatory visit—complete with autographs for the kids—from Phil Rizzuto. The wedding ceremony and luncheon the next day were to some of the fans—I mean, guests—almost superfluous.

No one seemed to care that the Yankees lost 6–1.

Ellen Shapiro

I recently bought a poster of Yankee Stadium. It is a 360-degree panoramic color photograph—the view you would see if you were sitting behind home plate, in the upper deck.

My work space is small; a cubicle I share with another editor, wide enough for two desks and a file cabinet. There is just enough room for the poster on the wall facing my desk. I can look out at the diamond and the green grass, the arches and the office buildings beyond. Now at work, listening to the conversations in the seats around me, I am there watching the action, soaking up the atmosphere of my favorite place.

Diane Lesniewski

Bobby Murcer is back with the Yankees as an announcer, and I am happy. Murcer was my boyhood idol, a lefty-hitting center fielder who wore number 1 on his back, whose bat looped lazily over his shoulders three times between each swing, whose hitting prowess might have won him a batting title one year were it not for a Twin named Oliva, and who was traded ignominiously to the Giants for Bobby Bonds. Blinded by rage and tears, I wrote a letter to manager Bill Virdon, demanding an explanation for his blasphemous trade of my hero. Now, listening to Murcer call the games, I am reminded of the joy and heartbreak of my baseball infancy. Knowing that he is still in pinstripes (figuratively, at least) makes my baseball adulthood that much more pleasant.

Joe Basile

This was told by Joel Oppenheimer, the late poet and sportswriter. At the time, Joel was covering the New York Mets for the Village Voice, *and he had heard it from the player involved.*

Casey Stengel was the Mets manager, and there was a pitcher on the team named Bob Shaw. Shaw never became much more than a journeyman pitcher, but he was known among his team-mates and other players as a notorious womanizer and a sharp dresser. He was usually the last to leave the dressing room after a game, as he prepared his sartorial stance for the night's activities.

One night Casey came into the dressing room and there was Shaw, standing in front of a mirror, primping. Casey went up to him. "Bob," he said. "Is it true you go out with a different woman every night?"

"That's right, Case. Every night, a new one."

Casey looked him right in the eye. "You must be a terrible f—k."

Paul Metcalf

I once went to a Red Sox-Yankees game with my parents and a friend of the family. I clearly remember him as a meek, quiet man nearing retirement age, someone who never showed his emotions. At some point in the game Ted Williams hit a home run and the place went wild. To my surprise, no one yelled louder or longer than our "quiet" friend. I'll never forget the sight of that stodgy old man suddenly brought to life; there he was, jumping up and down, clapping his hands, screaming with joy. At that moment he was a boy again, as young as I was. Nothing I have witnessed since has so strongly impressed upon me the ability of baseball, in its finest moments, to touch the child that survives in each of us.

Larry Baldassaro

Even before he clouted his historic homer, Bobby Thomson was my favorite player. One summer afternoon in the late forties, during pregame warmups at the Polo Grounds, I spotted him standing at the edge of the first base box seats, signing autographs. I jumped out of my grandstand seat, raced down the steep stairs, dodged a burly usher, ducked under a chain and finally reached him. Gasping for breath, hand shaking, I held out my scorecard. Bobby took it and quickly signed.

After the game and before the long drive home, my father and I stopped in the men's room. Before washing my hands, I set the program on a shelf over the sink. Halfway into the parking lot I felt a stab of agony. I turned and looked at the distant, now inaccessible ballpark, inside of which was a men's room with a sink and a shelf. And on the shelf, of course, was my priceless ten-cent scorecard with Bobby Thomson's autograph.

Christopher Jennison

It used to bother me that my brother's baseball stories, though entertaining and well-delivered, were never accurate. Now we're much older and I've realized that, when talking baseball, the facts become less important than good storytelling.

Mike Schacht

We were married on Christmas Eve, 1964, and went to Puerto Rico for our honeymoon. That Saturday afternoon we saw the Ponce Leones play the San Juan Senadores at Hiram Bithorn Stadium in San Juan.

Roberto Clemente was the player-manager of the home team. A young man sat next to us and quietly drank beer. Clemente's first hit was a double, followed by a single. The young man next to us quietly drank beer. Clemente's next hit was a home run, and as he limped around the bases the crowd cheered wildly. The young man next to us quietly drank beer.

As Clemente came in from right field, it was obvious that he was in pain. His fourth hit was a double and he took himself out of the game. As he limped across the infield the young man next to us lost control of himself. He jumped up in his seat and screamed, "Roberto Clemente is the son of God! He is Jesus Christ Himself reincarnated!"

Martha Blumberg

It is Christmas and I am watching a video of the seventh game of the 1952 World Series between the Yankees and the Dodgers. Roy Campanella is catching for Brooklyn. Lopat is pitching for the Yankees. There's Bauer, Berra, Mantle, Reese, Robinson, and Casey Stengel. Mel Allen is announcing that every pitch counts toward a winner's share of $2,300. Uniforms are baggy, socks are high, and the signs around the ballpark take me back to a city that is proud and strong.

It is fitting that I watch this game today. It is Christmas, but for me it is the end of a week of mourning for my father. I had just spoken with him to wish him happy birthday and talk endlessly about our usual topic—baseball. Later that same night I learned that he had died.

At the graveside service the following Sunday, the rabbi spoke of the loss of a great baseball fan and of the joy the game had brought to him. I had brought with me a small piece I had written about my father for an issue of *Fan.* It spoke of a difficult relationship that was healed through a shared love of baseball. I quietly slipped the copy into my father's grave.

Linda Ayache

At this point in my life I'm sliding into home plate, racing the ball to the catcher's mitt with all my strength and power. And it doesn't really matter what the call is because I feel safe in my performance.

Tony Palladino

My last visit to Tiger Stadium was a night game when I was eight years old. My father had come home from work and invited me to go with him. He was a fan and he took me to a number of games. He would talk to strangers around us or to other friends who had come with us, but he never talked much to me at those games.

In the second inning it started to rain. Very quickly it became a downpour. We took shelter under the stands for more than an hour, waiting in silence for the rain to stop. Finally, my father said that the rain had let up and we would make a run for the car, parked on Michigan Avenue.

Our car was a black '46 Ford sedan with a door on the driver's side that a key would not unlock. We arrived at the passenger's door dripping wet. As my father fumbled with the keys, he dropped them in the gutter. When he bent down to fish them out of the rushing water, the door handle knocked his brown fedora from his head. I caught up to the hat in about half a block.

When I returned to the car he was in the driver's seat and the passenger door was ajar. I jumped in and collapsed on the seat, dutifully handing him the hat, which now looked like a wet paper bag. He took it, stared at it for a split second, then put it on his head. Water dripped off the brim onto his shoulders and lap, the steering wheel and dashboard. Suddenly, he burst into a roar.

At first I was frightened because I thought he was howling with anger. When I realized he was laughing, I too became hysterical. I never heard my father laugh like that, before or after that night. It was a raw explosion that came from somewhere deep inside, something that he kept damned up.

Many years later, when I recalled that night and his laughter, he insisted that it never happened.

Stanly J. Benkoski

Girls didn't play baseball thirty years ago where I grew up. Girls weren't supposed to be athletes then; the closest we got was cheerleading. We went to the Little League fields and watched out brothers and their friends hit and field and spit and scratch and swear, and we told each other it was gross. But we always went back, every Friday night, to watch them.

I now have two sons who play on Little League and Pony League teams. They have their own gloves, and uniforms with their names on the back. They hit and field and scratch and spit and swear. When I see them in their uniforms, knocking the mud from their spikes at the plate, adjusting their batting stances with all the histrionics and seriousness of the pros, when one of them cries in the outfield after striking out, when the other has to be carried off the field after being hit by a pitch, when I see one of them touching third on his way home, see how he tries to hide that look of pride and triumph, that's when I long to rewrite the rules of my childhood.

Lisa Chewning

Mike Schacht

The box seats, the first ever for me, courtesy of my older brother, home on leave, were down the left-field line at Ebbets Field, right next to the visitors' bullpen. The Cards were in town and I got to see Ted Wilks and Harry Brecheen close up. That was good enough for me. But things got better.

Whitey Kurowski lined a foul ball my way and, after a few bounces and skips, that ball landed at my feet. And I grabbed it. But not for long, because you had to throw the balls back in 1944—part of the war effort. I held it. I clutched it. I could not throw that ball back. It was stuck in my hand forever. Ushers were closing in and I felt like a dead-end kid in a Cagney movie, so I panicked and threw the ball into short left field to Jocko Conlan, the umpire.

William Lucano

Jonathan is five,
and growing;
especially in sports.
Baseball is his favorite
and he insists on playing
with the others.

So what if he runs
to the pitcher's mound,
or in the wrong direction,
instead of to first base.
That he fights with
his teammates
in the outfield over
who should keep or catch
or roll the ball.

That he does handstands
and will pile up dirt
in the infield.

Deloris Selinsky

Our first shirt-sleeve day of spring
and I've puddle jumped
all twelve blocks home from school
to find my
big brother John my
hero my
buddy
grinnin' in our soggy front yard
at that girl,
that goofy Susie Miller,
lobbin' underbelly soft curves to her with
our still-in-the-box baseball
laughin' when she
squeaks away from his sissy tosses
and bats at them in the air with
my glove
my
glove
How could he?

Trish Mileham

Y ou have to catch the wind to let a home run begin.

Irene Lagorio

T alent against talent against fate.

Bruce Ario

Willie & Ernie
Meet on the Street

S ay Hey!
let's play

It's a great day!
let's do
two

Graham Wilcox

They're ripping up the old ball field today
The place where we first felt the sting of cold
Early springs and balls hit off the inside of the bat
Where you were Mickey and I was Willie

Timothy W. Kurth

I was sitting in Fenway Park with my Uncle Tim the day Jim Hegan gave me a baseball. It could have been '54; it could have been a year or two later. Hegan, a friend of my uncle's, caught the extraordinary Cleveland pitching staffs of the late 1940s and 1950s.

We were on the third-base side, near the visitors' dugout, in the front row. Hegan had just finished warming up Cleveland's ace, Bob Feller. The game was about to begin when he sidled over to us and leaned against the waist-high barrier. All the while he seemed to gaze across home plate toward the Red Sox dugout.

Earlier, Tim had introduced me and the two men had exchanged pleasantries. Now, near game time, Hegan was more on edge. He placed his glove along the top of the barrier, still staring off as if counting people in the crowd. "Here's something for your nephew," he said out of the side of his mouth.

Later, Tim told me of a rule forbidding players to fraternize with fans. It had to do with gambling, he said. So Tim cupped his hands beneath Hegan's big glove and the ball fell into them. "Here," my uncle said to me. "Don't lose it."

The ball Jim Hegan had used to warm up a Hall of Famer—a collector's item, an heirloom. A heartbreak . . . because I did lose it.

David W. Johnson

When I was seven years old my father went to Venezuela to work for an oil company, leaving my mother and me and my little sister.

He was gone for almost a year. The day he came back I went down the block to play baseball with my friends. As I came up to bat I could see my father, standing on the sidewalk in his suit and tie, watching. He was back, but he still seemed far away. My sister, upon seeing him, had been so frightened that she had cried. I wanted to impress him, so I swung hard and viciously at the pitches. I struck out and my father walked back to the apartment and never said anything about it to me.

Louis Phillips

One night after the 1939 season, during dinner with some friends in Minneapolis, I had occasion to ask Ted Williams two questions about his rookie season with Boston. I asked him, Who was the best pitcher you faced? And he said Ted Lyons. Then I asked him, Who was the best hitter you saw? And he said Charlie Gehringer.

Then he stood up in front of us and took a batting stance and said, "But no pitcher on earth can stop me from hitting."

He was only twenty-one at the time, but I guess that was pretty much prophetic.

David Thomas

I have taken enough young children to enough ball games to know that the play of the game itself is of irregular interest to them. There are so many other attractions bright with color and alive with noise: the vendors with their hot dogs and ice cream; the scoreboard with its flashing lights. By comparison, the game moves in stately progression, and its outbursts of activity are difficult for a child to follow.

But batting practice! Do not fail to take in batting practice. Half a dozen balls are in play at once among dozens of uniformed athletes who hit, field, run, and throw in concurrent but separate activity. It is not the game, but it is most emphatically baseball, and children delight in it.

My daughter was three years old at her initiation. For a week before the game, I emphasized our need to get out to the park early and catch warm-ups. "Gonna be the first ones in the park, get a good seat to watch the warm-ups." And on the day: "Let's get going, we don't want to miss the warm-ups."

So we caught the warm-ups. Then the game began, and progressed in its unhurried way, and in the fourth inning Elinor turned to me and said, "Dad, do you think the ball is warm yet?"

Eric Rolfe Greenberg

W e lived on a forty-acre tract on the edge of Beaver Crossing, Nebraska, a town of maybe four hundred people. The city park was just three blocks south, with a baseball diamond and grandstand, but there was no organized baseball for kids in Beaver Crossing. Some kids played there, but more would come play at our place, in the barnyard. It was a large barnyard, pretty flat, with home plate near the barn door and a squatty silo in short left field. Straight away center field might have been five hundred feet. All spring and summer we played ball in the barnyard. No coaches, no teachers, no grown-ups.

William Ahlschwede

I was born on Opening Day 79 years ago.
I realize there will not always be another April.

Graham Wilcox

When i was thirteen,
    i walked into
        the store
and asked for a bike

supporter. the man
    poked among the
        boxes
and gave me a kick

stand. i needed one,
    so i bought it
        with all
the money i had.

H.R. Coursen

Did you Know

Y ou could smoke a baseball?
You can also hit a rope up the middle.
A rope and a seed, as far as hitting one up the middle,
are actually synonymous.
A long drive has nothing to do with an automobile,
a dinger nothing to do with a bell.
The opposite of real grass is not fake grass
but Astro Turf. A pitcher pitches the ball,
a catcher catches the ball
but what does a shortstop do?
Bullpens corral
no cattle. They're home for closers
and long men.
Walls are called fences, fences

screens. Stealing is not only legal
but encouraged.
Running home is not a sign of immaturity.

Managers dress like players,
3 and 2 is not 5
but a full count.
Fair balls are no paler
than foul balls.
A base on balls
is not a base on balls
but four pitches out of the strike zone.
You stand with a bat in your hand
as you sit on a pitch.

Peter Spiro

It is not such a strange thing to admit that my father is responsible for my love of baseball. But my father was over fifty when I was born. He was a French-schooled, Harvard-educated scholar of Shakespeare, and an incessant quoter of obscure poetry. Yet somewhere along the way he got it into his head that it was his duty to give his only son the experience of this thing called Baseball. Though he had never played the game he signed up to coach my pre-Little League team.

He approached his coaching assignment as if he were researching a thesis. He began watching games on TV and listening to them on radio. He asked questions of anyone he thought might have a particular slant on the sport. He bought an assortment of books. He demonstrated diagrams of stances and positions. He studied, absorbed and began to form his own unique view of the game. And he began to love it.

I remember after practice sessions we would all sit in a circle at his feet and listen to him talk about the game as he saw it. He was like a born-again believer with a solemn fervor and a gift for instruction. He talked about the tradition of the game and said things like, "Now, do your best, but have fun. The clever men who fostered this game had fun in mind. Do not stray far from that. Try hard and play clean. If you succeed up there at the bat, fine. But whatever happens, you'll learn a little bit more."

I suppose it seems unlikely that seven year olds who just wanted to play ball and get dirty could possibly listen to such a man, but we did. We listened and learned.

After that season he didn't coach again, though he remained a faithful fan of the game. As I grew up he always came to watch me play, though his health began to deteriorate. Up until his death, when I was seventeen, there existed an unspoken bond between us. I'm sure it had a lot to do with our "discovery" of the game at the same time, but I think it was something more. I believe that for that season we were a typical father and son. Baseball helped him become something more than simply an intellectual, formal, older man confused as to how to relate.

It wasn't until much later that I realized that the most important things I learned that summer happened because my dad was anything but typical.

Bill Gaythwaite

Under the glare of an August sun,
Dad slid into third.
Long khaki pants were brakes
For his long pale body.
Still, he wrenched the bag
From its moorings,
Safe with a smile.

His derring-do on the basepaths surprised me,
Standing stunned at shortstop for the sons
Close enough to see him look up at the team of
Fathers in the dugout, grin at them hugely, and
Laugh enormously at 6'2", 210,

Surprised I was, because in my eight years

We had never even had a catch, father to son.

I had a twin brother instead.

And Dad swung the bat

In pre-Ruthian style, almost all forearms,

Not because he was pre-Ruthian himself, though.

He just didn't handle a bat well.

But today, having plowed powerfully around second

On a teammate's line single to right,

Taking a big risk,

My dad slid into third.

Peter J. Greenhill

Everyone Has a Baseball Story

So many things in life relate to baseball. If you or someone you know has a baseball-related experience or memory you would like to share in a future book of Mudville Diaries, please contact me at the following address:

Mike Schacht

Mudville Diaries

P.O. Box #7643

Atlanta, Georgia 30357-0643